What Starts in an Egg?

FIRST EDITION
Series Editor Penny Smith; **Art Editor** Leah Germann; **US Editors** Elizabeth Hester, John Searcy;
DTP Designer Almudena Díaz; **Pre-Production Producer** Nadine King; **Producer** Sara Hu;
Picture Research Myriam Megharbi; **Dinosaur Consultant** Dougal Dixon;
Reading Consultant Linda Gambrell, PhD

THIS EDITION
Editorial Management by Oriel Square
Produced for DK by WonderLab Group LLC
Jennifer Emmett, Erica Green, Kate Hale, *Founders*

Editors Grace Hill Smith, Libby Romero, Michaela Weglinski;
Photography Editors Kelley Miller, Annette Kiesow, Nicole DiMella;
Managing Editor Rachel Houghton; **Designers** Project Design Company;
Researcher Michelle Harris; **Copy Editor** Lori Merritt; **Indexer** Connie Binder; **Proofreader** Larry Shea
Reading Specialist Dr. Jennifer L. Albro; **Curriculum Specialist** Elaine Larson

Published in the United States by DK Publishing
1745 Broadway, 20th Floor, New York, NY 10019

Copyright © 2023 Dorling Kindersley Limited
DK, a Division of Penguin Random House LLC
22 23 24 25 26 10 9 8 7 6 5 4 3 2 1
001-333884-May/2023

All rights reserved.

Without limiting the rights under the copyright reserved above, no part of this publication may be reproduced, stored in a
introduced into a retrieval system, or transmitted, in any form, or by any means (electronic, mechanical, photocopying,
recording, or otherwise), without the prior written permission of the copyright owner.
Published in Great Britain by Dorling Kindersley Limited

A catalog record for this book
is available from the Library of Congress.
HC ISBN: 978-0-7440-7155-9
PB ISBN: 978-0-7440-7156-6

DK books are available at special discounts when purchased in bulk for sales promotions, premiums,
fundraising, or educational use. For details, contact: DK Publishing Special Markets,
1745 Broadway, 20th Floor, New York, NY 10019
SpecialSales@dk.com

Printed and bound in China

The publisher would like to thank the following for their kind permission to reproduce their images:
a=above; c=center; b=below; l=left; r=right; t=top; b/g=background

Alamy Stock Photo: Erika Antoniazzo 22cra, Bel 19br, Blickwinkel / Agami / A. Audevard 9tr, Kike Calvo 19clb, D. Hurst 6bc
Gerry Pearce 8-9, Tom Stack 13bl; **Dreamstime.com:** Violeta Jahnel Brosig 21br, 23clb, Donyanedomam 18, Foryouinf 20br
Kerry Hargrove 10br, Elizabeth Hoffmann 4-5, Brett Hondow 3cb, 7b, Kwiktor 8br, Sander Meertins 16bl,
Randall Runtsch 18clb, Spiroview Inc. 18br, 22br, Steveheap 11clb, Tirrasa 7clb, 23cla, Lukas Vejrik 14-5, Gale Verhague 10bl
23tl, Dmitry Zhukov 17br; **Getty Images:** imageBROKER / Friedhelm Adam 16-17, Stone / Paul Starosta 17c,
The Image Bank / Jason Edwards 20-21; **Getty Images / iStock:** BirdImages 23bl, Emirhan Karamuk 21bl, Leonello 14br,
Thorsten Spoerlein 19, 22cl, Steve-K 17bl; **naturepl.com:** Fred Bavendam 12-13, Juergen Freund 15cb, 23cl,
Doug Gimesy 15bl; **Shutterstock.com:** 3DMI 12br, Stacey Ann Alberts 5t, Eric Isselee 9bc, 9br, Konstantin Novikov 13bc,
Phugunfire 9bl; **U.S.F.W.S:** James Kawlewski 10-11, Grayson Smith 11br

Cover images: *Front:* **Dreamstime.com:** Macrovector c; Getty Images / iStock: Liana2012l;
Back: **Dreamstime.com:** Dannyphoto80 clb, Godruma cra; **Getty Images / iStock:** DigitalVision Vectors / gollykim cla

All other images © Dorling Kindersley
For more information see: www.dkimages.com

For the curious
www.dk.com

What Starts in an Egg?

Ruth A. Musgrave

These are eggs.
Some eggs are
very big.
This bird came
from an egg.

egg

ostrich

4

Some eggs are very small. Bugs come out of these eggs.

ladybug

Some eggs are pretty colors. What color are these eggs?

southern cassowary
[CAS-sa-ware-ee]

eggs

9

killdeer

Some eggs are hard to see. Can you find three eggs in the rocks?

Some eggs are in the ocean. This animal came from an egg.

giant Pacific octopus

eggs

This animal came from an egg, too.
Mom curls around her eggs to keep them safe.

platypus

eggs

Some eggs look different. But they all have a baby that grows inside.

map butterfly

eggs
17

All eggs have a shell. Some shells are hard. Some are soft.

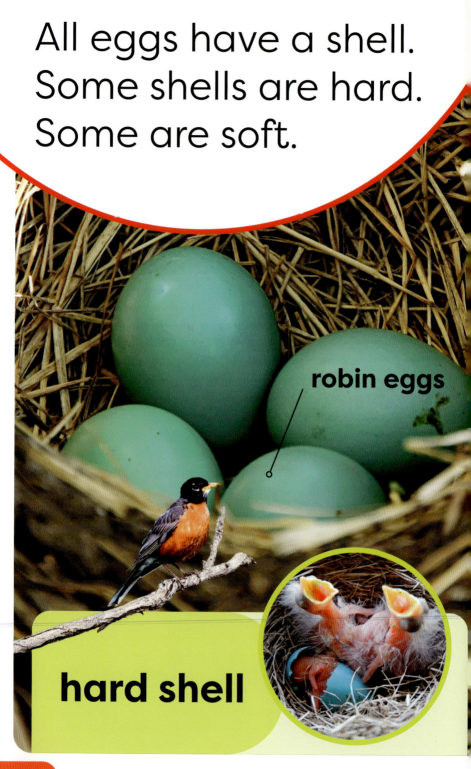

robin eggs

hard shell

The baby is ready to leave the egg. It breaks out of the shell.

sea turtle

Happy birthday, babies!

22

Glossary

killdeer
a bird that adds rocks and sticks to its nest to hide the eggs

ladybug
an insect that eats other smaller insects

platypus
a river animal with a bill and webbed feet like a duck

sea turtle
a sea animal that lays its eggs on the beach

southern cassowary
a tall, heavy bird that does not fly

Quiz

Answer the questions to see what you have learned. Check your answers with an adult.

1. What animal's eggs look like rocks?
2. Which animal comes from an egg in the ocean?
3. Which animal mom curls around her eggs?
4. What is the outside of an egg called?
5. True or False: All eggs have a hard shell.

1. Killdeer eggs 2. Giant Pacific octopus 3. Platypus
4. Shell 5. False